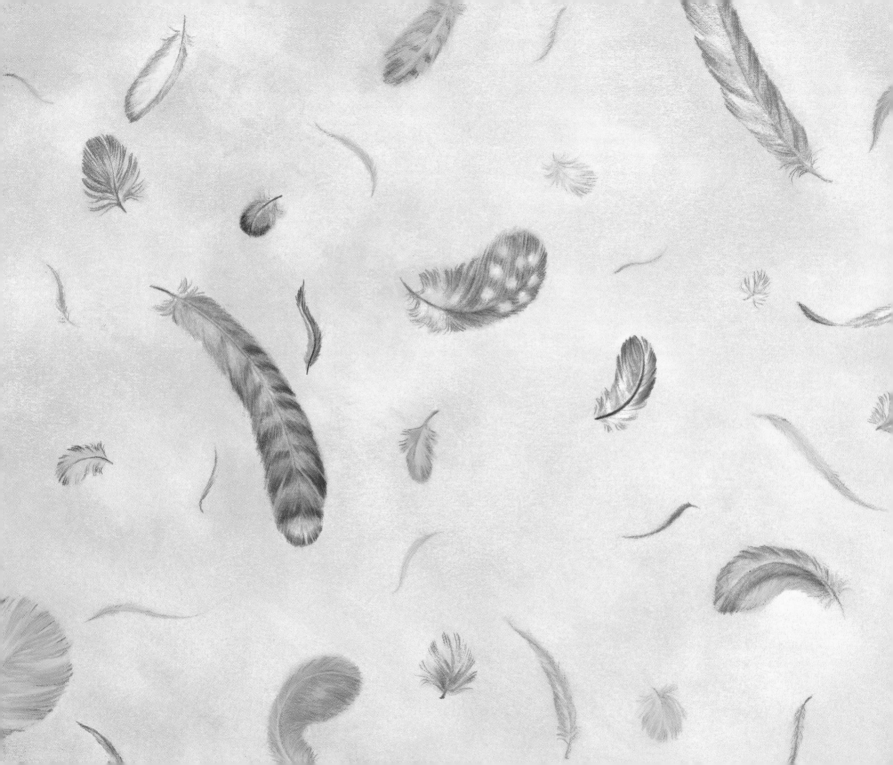

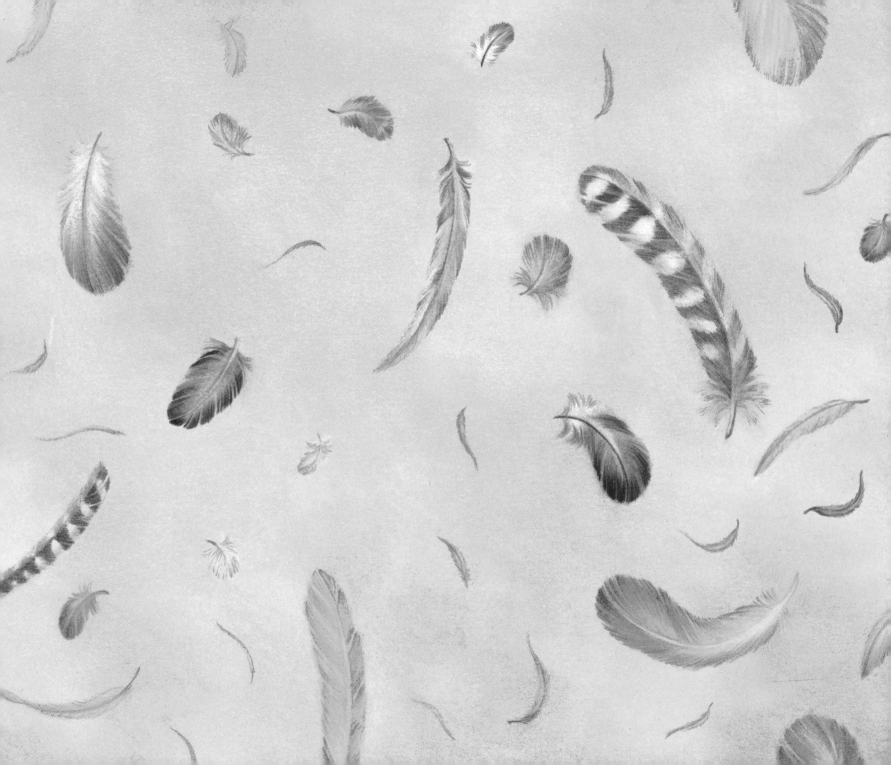

LET'S·READ·AND·FIND·OUT SCIENCE®

STAGE 2

Did Dinosaurs Have Feathers?

By Kathleen Weidner Zoehfeld

Illustrated by Lucia Washburn

HarperCollins*Publishers*

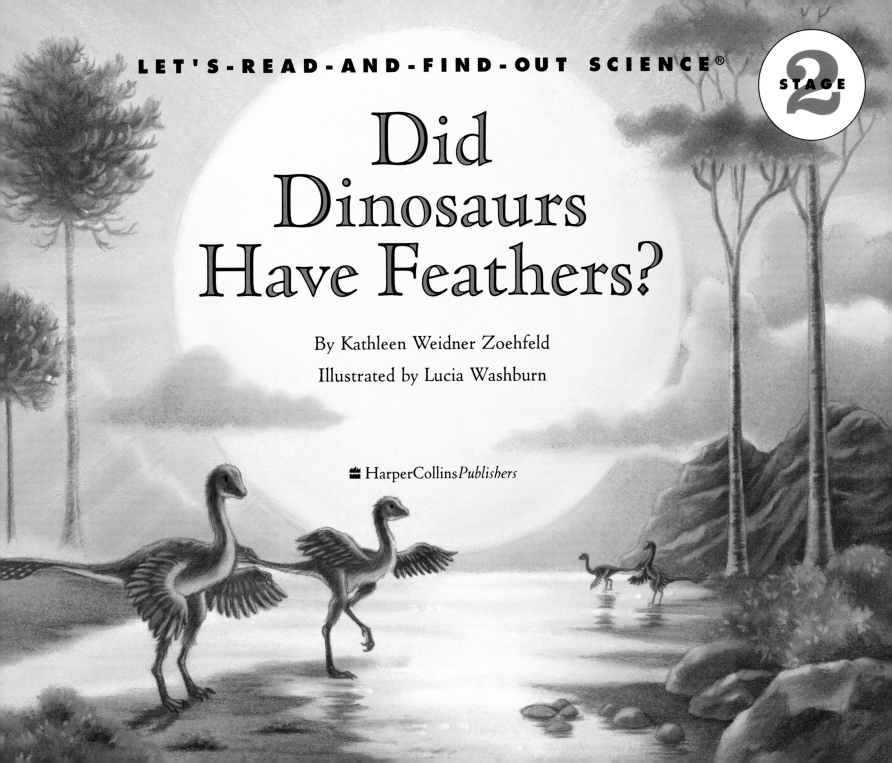

For Bruce
—*K. W. Z.*

For our golden-feathered Sequoia
—*L. W.*

Special thanks to
Dr. Robert T. Bakker
for his time and expert review.

The *Let's-Read-and-Find-Out Science* book series was originated by Dr. Franklyn M. Branley, Astronomer Emeritus and former Chairman of the American Museum–Hayden Planetarium, and was formerly co-edited by him and Dr. Roma Gans, Professor Emeritus of Childhood Education, Teachers College, Columbia University. Text and illustrations for each of the books in the series are checked for accuracy by an expert in the relevant field. For more information about Let's-Read-and-Find-Out Science books, write to HarperCollins Children's Books, 1350 Avenue of the Americas, New York, NY 10019, or visit our website at www.letsreadandfindout.com.

HarperCollins®, ♣ ®, and Let's Read-and-Find-Out Science®
are trademarks of HarperCollins Publishers Inc.

Library of Congress Cataloging-in-Publication Data
Zoehfeld, Kathleen Weidner.
Did dinosaurs have feathers? / by Kathleen Weidner Zoehfeld ; illustrated by Lucia Washburn.—1st ed.
p.   cm. — (Let's-read-and-find-out science. Stage 2)
Summary: Discusses the discovery and analysis of Archaeopteryx, a feathered dinosaur which may have been an ancestor of modern birds.
ISBN 0-06-029026-9 — ISBN 0-06-029027-7 (lib. bdg.) — ISBN 0-06-445218-2 (pbk.)
1. Archaeopteryx—Juvenile literature. [1. Archaeopteryx. 2. Dinosaurs.] I. Washburn, Lucia, ill. II. Title.   III. Series.
QE872.A8Z64 2004 2002010585 568'.22—dc21

Typography by Elynn Cohen   1 2 3 4 5 6 7 8 9 10   ❖   First Edition

Did
Dinosaurs
Have Feathers?

All birds have feathers. They have short, fluffy feathers. And they have feathers that are smooth and long.

On chilly days, fluffy feathers keep birds warm.

Long, smooth flight feathers on their wings help birds get off the ground. They flap their feathered wings to fly and stretch them out to soar.

Bright, colorful feathers help birds know each other. Quiet colors can help them hide themselves from enemies.

Birds are the only living animals with feathers. But there was a time in Earth's history when there were no birds. Two hundred thirty million years ago, the first dinosaurs began to appear on Earth. There were no birds then, and no animals with feathers.

So where did birds come from? And how did their amazing feathers develop?

8

One of the oldest feathers we know about belonged to a creature that lived 145 million years ago—about 85 million years after the earliest dinosaurs.

All feathers are delicate. None can last for 145 million years. But long ago, this feather fell into fine-grained mud. As the mud hardened into rock, it preserved a perfect print of the feather.

This beautiful two-and-a-half inch fossil print was discovered in 1860 in Solnhofen, Germany. The German scientist Hermann von Meyer named the creature the feather came from. He called it *Archaeopteryx,* or "ancient wing."

Very soon after that, an *Archaeopteryx* skeleton
was found, complete with prints of feathers on its
wings and tail. Since von Meyer's time, six more
Archaeopteryx fossils have been discovered.

Archaeopteryx had feathers. But was it a bird?
Archaeopteryx does not look quite like the birds we know!
For one thing, it had teeth. No living birds have teeth.
And it had a long, bony tail. Today's birds have short tails.
Some may have long tail feathers, but their tailbones are small
and stubby.

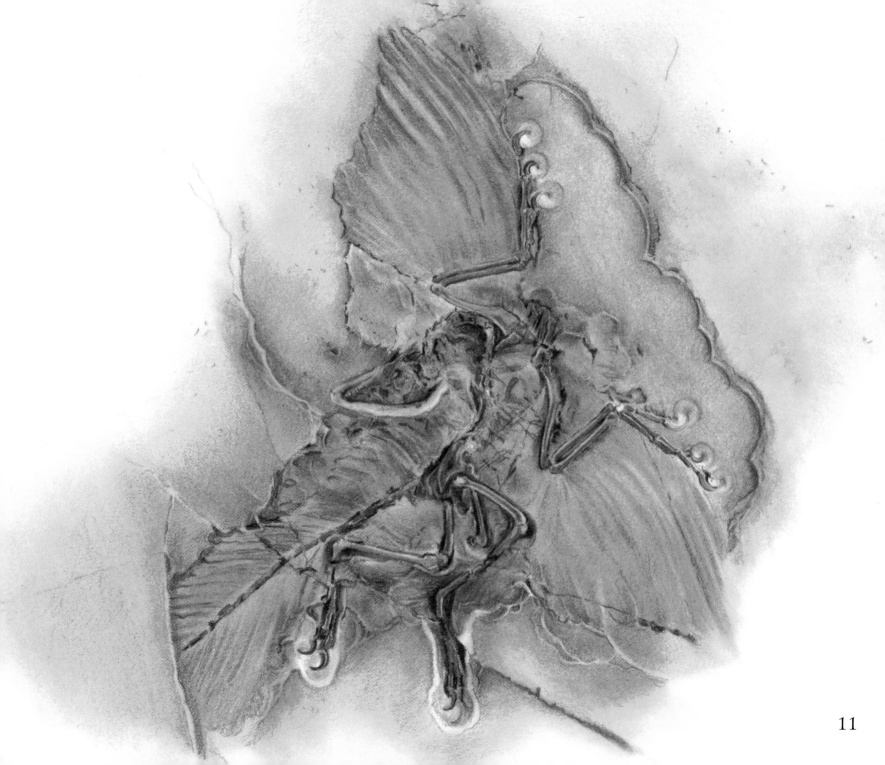

11

Archaeopteryx's wings and feathers looked like those of modern birds. In fact, many scientists think *Archaeopteryx* was able to fly. But unlike birds, *Archaeopteryx* had three long, clawed fingers on the front edge of each wing.

Archaeopteryx had the wings and feathers of a bird, but its sharp teeth, long tail, and clawed hands were very much like a dinosaur's. So what *was* this newly discovered feathered creature? Dinosaur or bird?

In the 1860s, scientists decided to call *Archaeopteryx* Earth's oldest, or first, bird. Nevertheless, many believed that this weird bird must have developed from dinosaur ancestors.

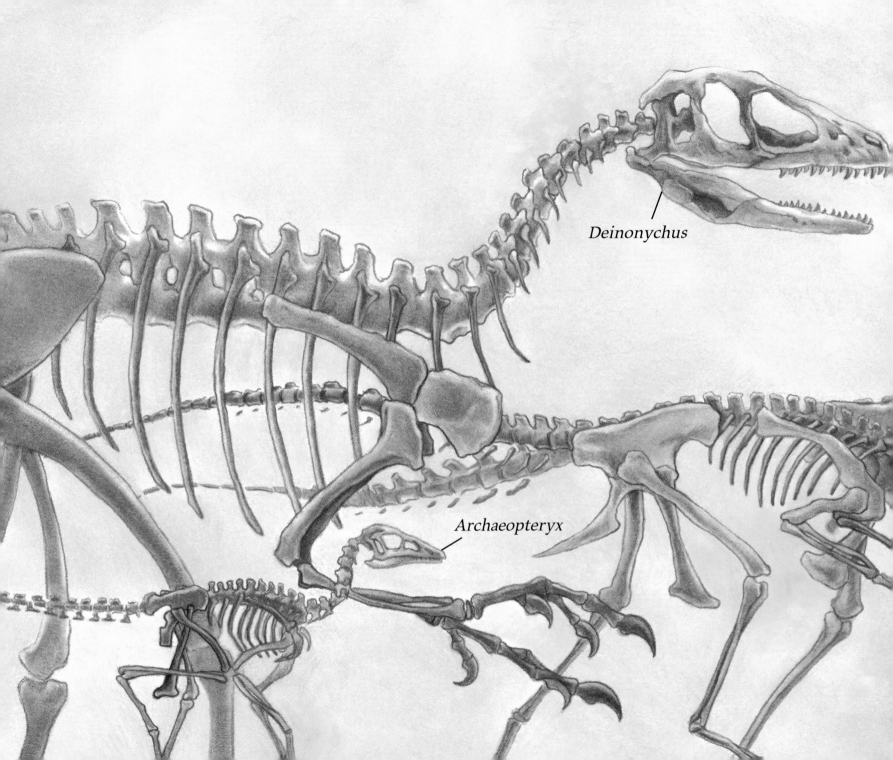

Deinonychus

Archaeopteryx

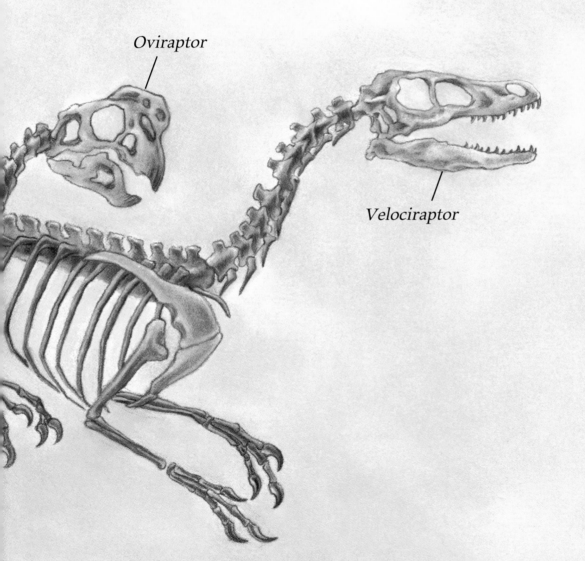

Oviraptor

Velociraptor

Over years of careful study, scientists have discovered that _Archaeopteryx's_ bones are very similar to the bones of meat-eating dinosaurs. Meat-eating dinosaurs make up the group of dinosaurs called theropods.

The theropod group includes some of the fiercest and most famous of all dinosaurs—the huge _Tyrannosaurus_ and the smaller _Deinonychus, Oviraptor,_ and _Velociraptor._

15

Theropod dinosaurs walked on two legs
and had three-toed feet, with claws, just as
birds do. Both theropods and birds
have S-shaped necks and light, hollow
bones.

Birds have wishbones that give their wings much of the strength they need to fly. Some theropod dinosaurs also had wishbones.

Birds have feathers. And so did *Archaeopteryx*. Scientists wondered if some theropod dinosaurs might have had feathers, too.

It takes rare and special conditions for delicate feathers to fossilize. So, even if a dinosaur did have feathers, in most cases they would not be preserved.

Once in a while, though, feathers do leave fossil prints. That's how we can be sure that *Archaeopteryx* and at least a few theropods did indeed have feathers.

In the 1990s, scientists in China's Liaoning Province discovered an area rich in fossils. The fossils were about 145 to 125 million years old, and they were preserved in rocks as fine grained as those in Solnhofen, Germany.

In 1996, Ji Qiang, the director of the National Geological Museum in Beijing, received a particularly interesting fossil from a Liaoning farmer. It was a small theropod dinosaur, about the size of a chicken. It had sharp teeth, short arms with clawed hands, long legs, and a long, bony tail.

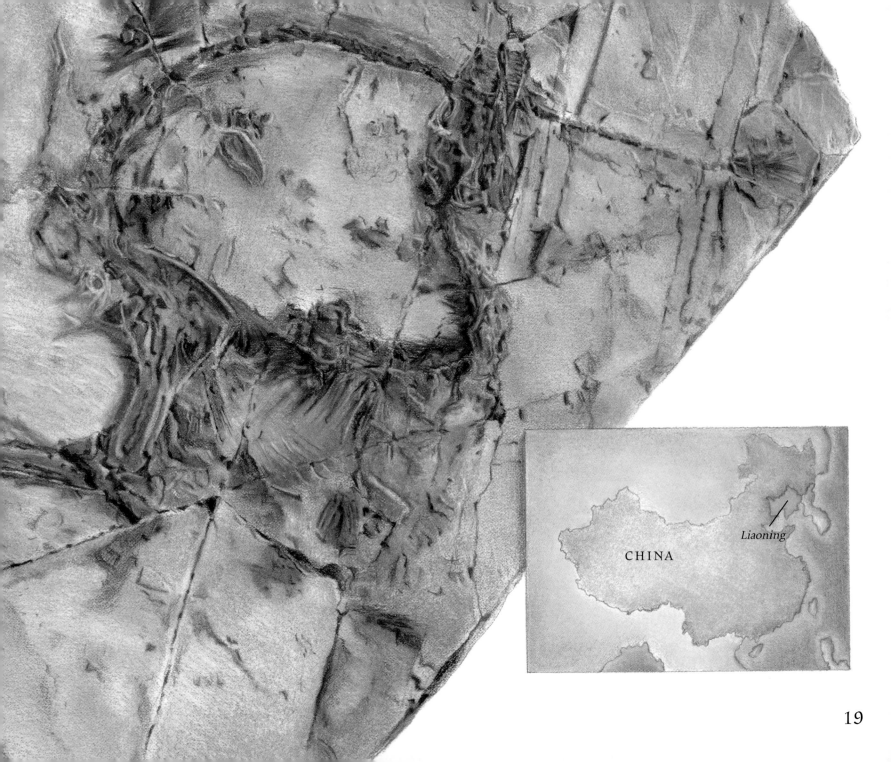

CHINA

Liaoning

19

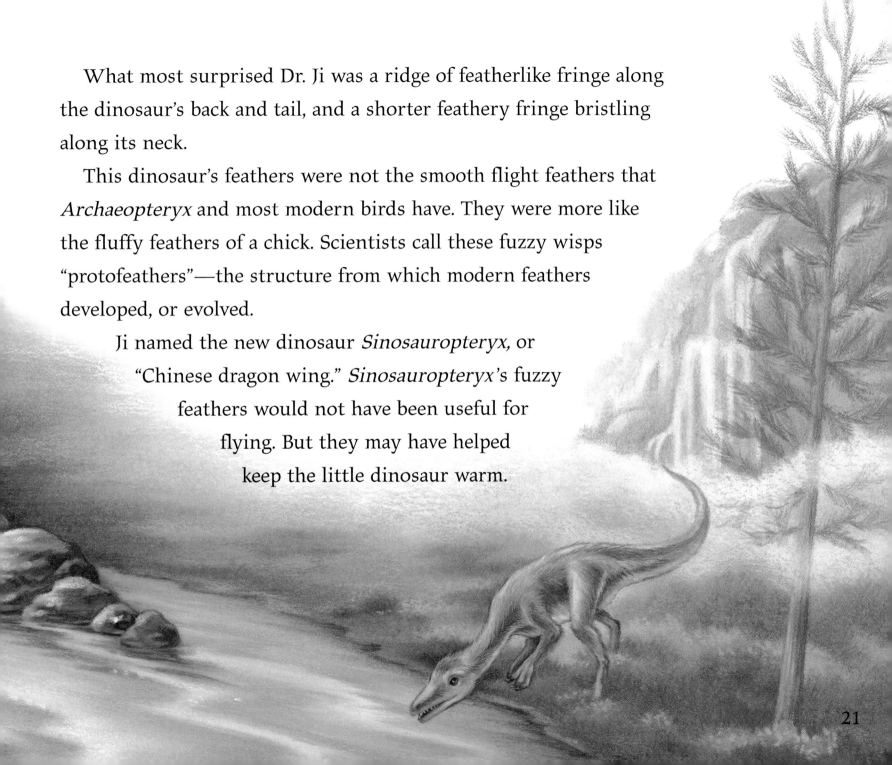

What most surprised Dr. Ji was a ridge of featherlike fringe along the dinosaur's back and tail, and a shorter feathery fringe bristling along its neck.

This dinosaur's feathers were not the smooth flight feathers that *Archaeopteryx* and most modern birds have. They were more like the fluffy feathers of a chick. Scientists call these fuzzy wisps "protofeathers"—the structure from which modern feathers developed, or evolved.

Ji named the new dinosaur *Sinosauropteryx,* or "Chinese dragon wing." *Sinosauropteryx*'s fuzzy feathers would not have been useful for flying. But they may have helped keep the little dinosaur warm.

21

Not long after the discovery of *Sinosauropteryx*, several other feathered theropods were unearthed in Liaoning. The turkey-sized *Protarchaeopteryx* and *Caudipteryx* had fuzzy protofeathers on their bodies. But they also had smooth feathers on their arms. And they each had a fan of feathers on their tails.

Perhaps, like today's turkeys, *Protarchaeopteryx* and *Caudipteryx* could have spread their fancy tail feathers to show off for their mates or to frighten their enemies.

The slightly larger and scarier *Sinornithosaurus* could flap its long, feathered arms. Much of its body was covered in thick, feathery fuzz. And its jaws were lined with sharp, deadly teeth.

Beipiaosaurus was one of the biggest feathered dinosaurs. It weighed as much as an ostrich and was over seven feet long.

Microraptor is one of the smallest dinosaurs ever found. It had smooth feathers on its arms and legs and tail. *Microraptor* was so small, you could have held it in your hands—that is, if you weren't afraid of its sharp bite!

Microraptor

Beipiaosaurus

Sinornithosaurus

25

Today most scientists believe that *Archaeopteryx* and all modern birds evolved from theropod dinosaurs.

Feathers probably first developed to keep small dinosaurs warm. Arm feathers may have helped them hatch their eggs. Colors and patterns on their feathers may have let dinosaurs recognize each other. Or they may have helped them hide.

Small dinosaurs with long feathers on their arms and legs could have glided from tree to tree. Some of the ancient feathered theropods may even have been able to flap their wings and fly.

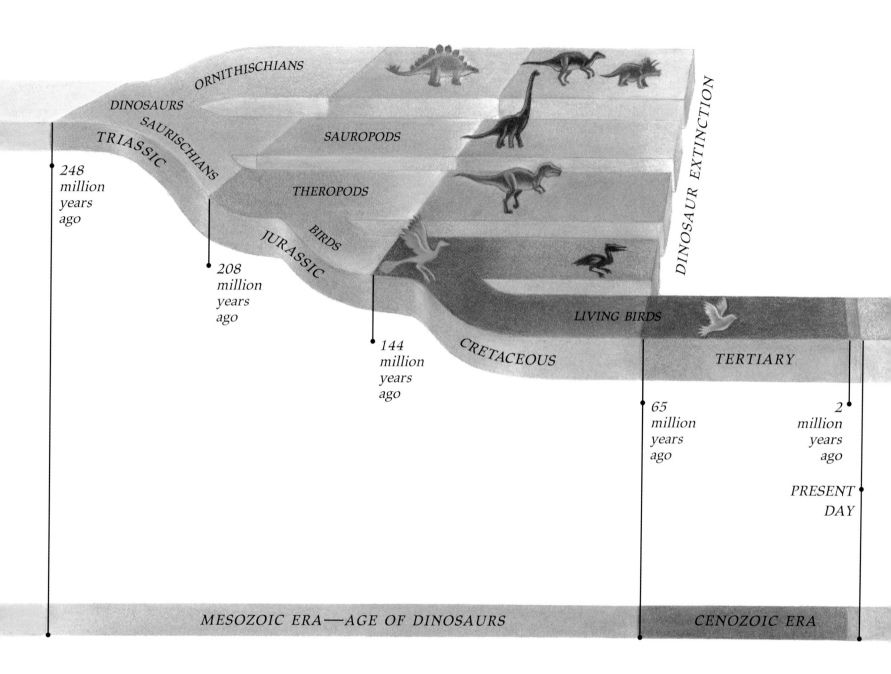

ORNITHISCHIANS

DINOSAURS

SAURISCHIANS

TRIASSIC

SAUROPODS

THEROPODS

BIRDS

JURASSIC

DINOSAUR EXTINCTION

248
million
years
ago

208
million
years
ago

144
million
years
ago

CRETACEOUS

LIVING BIRDS

TERTIARY

65
million
years
ago

2
million
years
ago

PRESENT
DAY

MESOZOIC ERA—AGE OF DINOSAURS

CENOZOIC ERA

Over the course of millions of years, a few theropod dinosaurs evolved to become more and more like the birds we know.

Sixty-five million years ago, a worldwide disaster caused dinosaurs to die out. But most scientists now agree that only the big, land-based dinosaurs became extinct. Many of the smaller ones that had evolved feathers and flight lived on.

The descendants of the feathered dinosaurs still soar through our skies every day. It's easy to find them. They're busy pecking for seeds at backyard bird feeders, diving for fish in rivers and seas, or weaving through the woods in search of little mammals to dine on, much the way their ancestors did, millions of years ago.

31

FIND OUT MORE ABOUT FEATHERS

What kinds of dinosaur feathers can you find in your own neighborhood?

Birds, our modern dinosaurs, shed or "molt" their worn-out feathers a few at a time. New feathers grow in to replace the old ones. As you walk to school, or while you play in your backyard or at the park, keep your eyes open for shed feathers.

Here are some different types to look for:

- Contour feathers—These are among the largest, stiffest feathers you will find. They give a bird's body its smooth outer covering. Birds' wings are lined with contour feathers that are specially shaped to give them lift when flying.

- Semiplume feathers—Smaller and more flexible than contour feathers, these feathers are soft and fluffy.

- Downy feathers—These are very small, light, fluffy feathers. Semiplume and downy feathers grow under the contour feathers and are designed to keep birds warm.

See if you can find feathers of different colors, or feathers with spots, stripes, or bars.

See the strong spine, or "shaft," of the feather, and notice the thousands of threadlike "barbs" attached to both sides of the shaft.

On contour feathers, most of the barbs cling to their neighbors like little zippers. On each barb, teensy hooks, called "barbules," do the zipping. All the barbs lying neatly together make a smooth "vane" on either side of the shaft.

Try separating the barbs gently with your fingers and then smoothing them together again.

You'll know semiplume and downy feathers when you see them. Their shafts are fine, and their barbs do not zip together. They stay all loose and fluffy.

Note: Rinse your feathers in warm water, let them dry, then put them in the microwave on high for one minute to get rid of the germs and tiny insect critters that may live on feathers found outdoors.

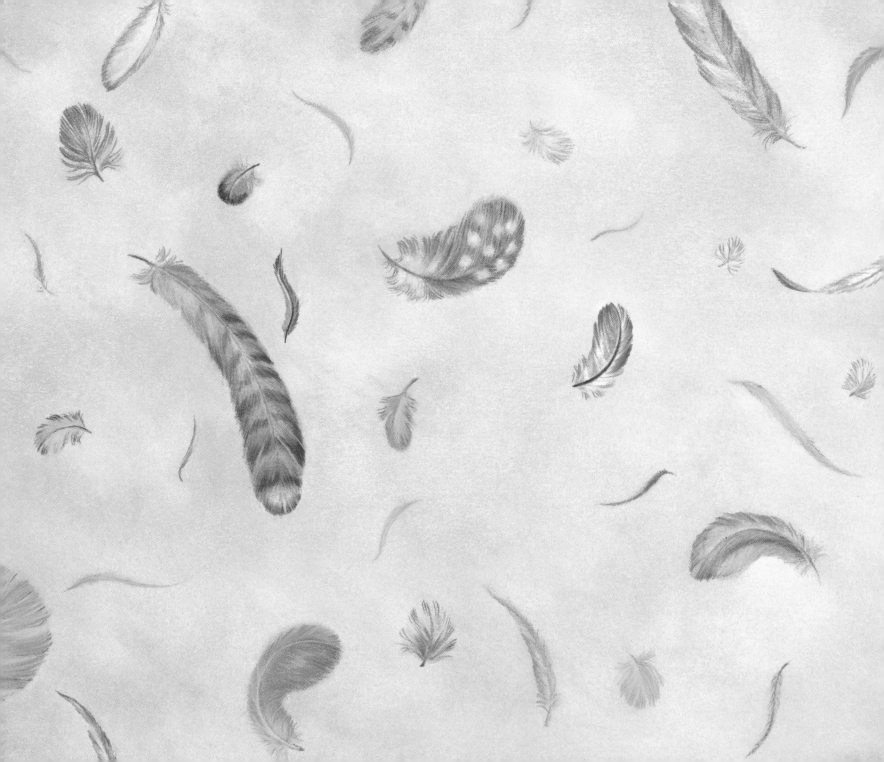

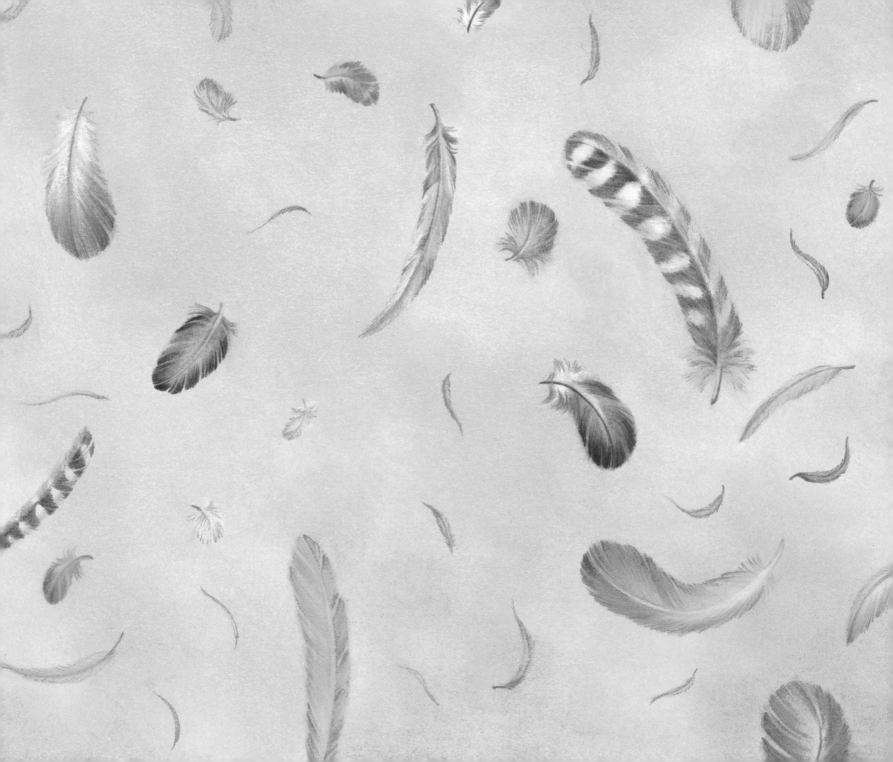